A Dictionary of Bristle

Third Edition

Harry Stoke and Vinny Green

For

Justin Lee Collins

A Bristolian oasis in a television desert

First Edition Published by Broadcast Books 2003

Second Edition Published by Broadcast Books 2005

Third Edition published by Tangent Books 2009, 2011, 2012

Tangent Books
Unit 5.16 Paintworks
Bristol
BS4 3EH

0117 972 0645

www.tangentbooks.co.uk

Copyright Tangent Books 2012
richard@tangentbooks.co.uk

ISBN 9781906477295

Cover design by
Ira Rainey

Printed in Great Britain by Short Run Press

Introduction

Introduction

Welcome to this, our third edition of *A Dictionary Of Bristle*: a unique collection of words, phrases, and pronunciations that started life as a simple tongue-in-cheek section from the award-winning satirical website *That Be Bristle*. But from small acorns grow large trees, as was proved by the runaway success of the first paperback edition of this dictionary.

Thanks to Bristolians throughout the city and around the world, who are proud of who they are and how they sound, we have been able to update and expand this humorous - yet curiously informative - insight into the strange-sounding language of the South West's capital city.

Bristolian is a distinctly warm-toned dialect that, like most regional variations of language, contains standard English words and phrases that mean something very different to its native speakers. In a city where a *drive* is somebody at the wheel and not something you do on a Sunday afternoon, and a *spanner* is never going to help you fix a car, life can easily get confusing for the unwary.

Bristolian also has words and pronunciations that are unique to the city which can often baffle people not familiar with the rolled R's, the dropped H's, and the addition of L's to the end of practically any word that ends in a vowel. As if that isn't potential enough to strike a look of bewilderment onto the face of a visitor, the unaided ear also has to deal with the confusion of ownership and tense, and the use of the personal pronoun *Ee* (he) for impersonal objects: "*Me ammer? Ee's over yer look.*"

Like all regional dialects though, Bristolian is in danger of dying out. With the large new suburbs of Bradley Stoke and Emersons Green attracting people to Bristol from all over the UK, the 30,000+ students that fill the universities each term, and the widening of new middle class enclaves gentrifying the housing of many former working areas of the city, from Bishopston and Horfield to Easton and Southville, the melting pot of language in the city is slowly diluting Bristol's true identity.

Yet even without this slim volume to fight its corner, the dialect still has its strongholds, notably in pockets of Bristol communities such as Southmead, Bedminster, Knowle West, and Hartcliffe. The language lives on, and with the help of this book, will continue to do so.

The aim of this dictionary is to collate words and phrases in common usage in and around Bristol, both past and present, in a bid to keep the Bristolian tongue alive. Some entries in this collection cross generations and some cross over into other regional dialects and general slang, but all are listed here if they play, or have played, a part in the makeup of Bristolian. You may not recognise them all - I've been a Bristolian since birth and some still surprise even me - but with the help of this Dictionary we hope that you'll soon be hearing - and understanding - a lot more of them.

Harry Stoke
Bristol, UK

Pronunciation

Pronunciation

An important test of Bristolian is that it's not only lazy in style but rhythmic as well, so that consonants are essential to achieve effortless delivery. No true Bristolian would use an iota more energy than they need to deliver a statement. As in the morning greeting on the workers' bus - *Awlrite 'arry? Awlrite, 'n thee?* No answer was required. Elegant economy.

There are several rules to Bristolian which shape its sound and flow and are essential to master if you want to learn to speak or understand Bristolian. Its use of *a*, *i*, *l*, *r*, *s*, *t*, and its lack of *h*, the pronunciation of *th* and *ing*, its confusion of ownership and tense, and its addition of words to the end of sentences. Also, harsh sounding letters and syllables are generally dropped or substituted for softer ones.

A An *a* located within a word is usually pronounced like the *a* in sat: a kind of drawn out *ahh* sound, giving words like *apple*, *glass*, and *bath* a distinct sound.

I *I* is very often used as both a subjective and an objective personal pronoun. This turns *Give it to me* into *Gif I it!* and *That's just like me* into *Thas just like I*.

L Words that end in a vowel often have a short *I* added to the end of them turning *area* into *aerial* and *idea* into *ideal*.

This mostly occurs when the next word begins with a vowel. However where words actually end with an *I* it is often silent. Where an *I* is pronounced it will generally be accompanied with an *aw* sound such as *Breakfast Cereawl*.

The letter *I* is also often inserted into words where the *aw* coupling exists such as *drawing* which becomes *drawlen*.

R   *r* is often heavily emphasised both at the start and ending of words with the sound of *er*, this gives them a warm tone, such as *NeveR*, *BabbeR* and *Right*.

S   *s* is usually added to the end of verbs when referring to all persons, instead of just the singular third person. This turns phrases like *I go* into *I goes* and *They go* into *They goes*.

T   Where a *t* is found inside a word it is rarely pronounced and if it is it will be very soft. This turns words like *Westbury* into *Wessbree*, *Weston* into *Wesson*, and even *Bristol* into *Bristle*.

H   Words that begin with *h* are shortened disregarding the first letter giving us *ave im* instead of *Have him*. This trait is also sometimes applied to the letter *w* as seen in *He would* turning into *Ee ood*.

TH   Where the coupling of *th* occurs at the start of a word it will often be pronounced as an *f* turning *think* into *fink*. This could also apply when it is found at the end of, or inside a word, but where this is the case it can also be pronounced as a *d* or a *v*, turning *with* into *wiv*.

ING   Where the triplet of *ing* occurs at the end of a word it is often pronounced as *en* with emphasis on the *n*, but be warned this is not always the case. Where this does occur it changes *Going raving?* into *Goen rave-en?* and *Are you going to do all the driving?* into *Is you gonna do all the drive-en?*

END To finish a sentence generally a choice of four words can be used; *Like*, *Look*, *Mind*, or *See*. Which word you use would depend upon the context of the sentence:

Like In place of *er*, when you pause for thought during a sentence.
You can ave im fer like, a fiver or summat

Look When you find something that's been lost.
Yer tis, look!

Mind When you're taking a full pint back to the table in the pub.
Be careful with that, mind!

See When you've proved yourself right in an argument.
I tawld you, see!

Dictionary

A
Of *or* To *or* The
*Canave one a they?/I ain't goen
back a work now.*

Aarsh
Harsh
Oo, that waz pretty aarsh!

**Ackrut/
Ackrutlee**
Accurate/Accurately
Ee casn't be as ackrut as I!

Aeriawl
A particular region
What aeriawl do ee live in?

Almunsbree
Almondsbury, a village to
the north of Bristol
*Yeah, thas up by Almunsbree
Inner Change.*

Ambag
Handbag
Seen me ambag muh?

Amblance
Ambulance
*Jew see that amblance what
whizzed past?*

Americawl
United States of America
I got ee over in Americawl mind.

Anneye	Haven't I *I only bleeden done it again anneye!*
Amt	Have not *I amt got it, I fink ar muh got it.*
Ank	To go fast (usually on two wheels of a four-wheeled vehicle) *Blige! Ee anked it rown that corner mind!*
Annum	Hanham, an area east of Bristol *or* Haven't they *They got some bigguns in Annam, annum!*
Annus	Haven't we *We both gotta get that bus ohm annus?*
Ansum	Handsome *Eeuz evsa ansum.*
Ant	Has not *Ee ant even ast us what weeda want!*
Anudder	Another *Gif I anudder one in ere me luv.*

A - Z

Any Rate   Anyway
She left I, but I dint like err any rate.

Appapie   Apple pie
Lav appapie an custurd.

Ar   Our
Ar muh said I was right.

Ar Muh   My / Our mother
Ar muh's maken tea.

Ar Ole Man   My / Our father
Ar ole man bin down a pub all day.

Ard   Tough / Violent
Ee's ard as nails ee is.

Ark   Look / Listen
Ark at ee.

Arrmen   As said at the end of a prayer
*Ar lord, who art in Soufmeed,
be nice to I. Arrmen.*

Arrtack   Heart Attack
*Ee ad arrtack on a bus - ee
wunt driven mind.*

Art Cleff	Hartcliffe, an area of South Bristol *Do this bus go up Art Cleff drive?*
Asdawl	A popular supermarket chain; Asda *Ar muh's down Asdawl at the minute.*
Assant	Haven't *Ee assant gone an broke it ave ee?*
Assaw	Asshole *Yer an assaw.*
Assit	That's it *Assit, right yer look.*
Ast	Ask *or* Have you *I ast err where Asdawl waz but she dint know/Ast ee seen me keys?*
Asthmawl	A restrictive breathing condition *I ain't gotta do games cause I got asthmawl.*
Astrawl	Vauxhall Astra *Seen they ali wills on is Astrawl?*

At

Had
Ee at a go down ar muh's ows.

Ater

After
Cas ee look ater ee fry?

Attle Avit

Had to have it
Once ee sawl it, ee attle avit.

Ave / Avin

Have / Having
Whas wonna ave fer tea?

Aves

Has
Ee aves to go a work urrlay mind.

Avvy

To beat somebody
I could avvy in a fight easy!

Awd

Old
Ow awd are you?

Awd Ee

Hold him / this / that
Cas ee awd ee while I gets anuver un.

Awdbree Coort   Oldbury Court Estate, an area of
                      East Bristol
                      They fown me car down
                      Awdbree Coort!

Awdeez   German budget supermarket
                      chain; Aldi
                      I got ee down Awdeez yeserday.

Awlful   Awful
                      Them bleeden pies is awlful.

Awlrite   Are you alright
                      Awlrite? Ow bis?

Awlrite Me Luvver? Hello, how are you my friend?
                      Awlrite me luvver? Ain't seen
                      you frages.

Awlun Common   Oldland Common, an area
                      east of Bristol
                      SBL? Thas down Awlun Common.

Awws   All I was
                      Awws tryin to do was elp err!

Babby / Babber Baby or Friend
*Don't be such a babby / Churz
me ole babber!*

Backee To carry a second person on a
pushbike
Gis I a backee ohm ullee?

Baff Bath, an affluent city south east of
Bristol
Iss posh out Baff mind!

Baity Riled / Annoyed
Ee was getten right baity.

Bammington A game played with shuttle
cock and racquet; Badminton
I plays bammington down ar club.

Bananawls Bananas
I bort some bananawls down Asdawl.

Banjo Island Park Estate, an area east of Bristol
Ave ee bin down Banjo safternun?

Bar Nil Barton Hill, an area of East Bristol
Eda live down Bar Nil in they flats.

Barawl Gurnee A former psychiatric hospital;
Barrow Gurney
Ee's a nutter. Ee awt a be in
Barawl Gurnee.

Basdurd Bastard
Yoom jus a basdurd, I ates you, I do!

Baws Testicles
Muh! Ar bruvver jus kicked I in
me baws!

Beamer Going red in the face with
embarrasment
Look at the gurt beamer on ee.

Bearpit A subterranean world at the back
of Debenhams
That Bearpit stinks a piss mind!

Bemmie / Bedmie A resident of Bedminster
You ain't a true Bemmie, yoom from up
Wimmilill.

Bemmie Down An area of South Bristol that
overlooks the Avon Gorge.
Ee cas see the spenshun bridge
from up Bemmie Down!

Bemminser

Bedminster, an area of
South Bristol
*Ar muh got err new tats done down
Bemminser – they'm gurt macky.*

Benny

To lose your temper
*Ee ad a right benny when I told im
bout me an err.*

Bide Still

Keep Still
Bide still ullee! Yoom doen me ead in!

Biggun

Big one
Ee's got a gurt biggun ee ave.

Bin

Been
Wheres bin?

Birfday

Birthday
Whas get me fer me birfday then?

Bis / Bist

Are you
Ow bist?

Bissen

Is not
Ee bissen gonna get nuffink out a I.

Blad	Useless idiot (derog.) *I ain't avin Stenner on my team, ee's a total blad.*
Blakforn	A popular alcoholic cider drink *Yer, that Blakforn's bleeden luvely!*
Bleenell	Bleeding Hell *Bleenell! I forgot me miat.*
Blige	Blimey *Blige! He didn't do that did ee?*
Borrawl	Borrow *Can I borrawl they shoes?*
Bort	Bought *I bort ee dowtown yeserday.*
Bout	About *Do ee know much bout it?*
Bovvered	Bothered *I int even bovvered what ee wants.*
Breckfuss	The first meal of the day; Breakfast *Muh, wheres me breckfuss?*

A - Z

Bristle / Brizzle   Bristol, the mother city
We luvs Bristle!

Briz   Brislington, an area of South Bristol
Ee ad a right eppy when ee was in Briz.

Brormeed   Broadmead, large shopping area in
central Bristol
Ar muh got ee fry down Brormeed.

Brung   Brought
I brung me own.

Bung   Put
Jus bung it down over yer.

Burmenam   Birmingham, a West Midlands city
Burmenam? Thas not rown yer mate.

Buzzer   Bumble Bee
I jus got stung by a bleeden buzzer!

Byerawl   Biro
Can I borrawl yer byerawl.

Cabry Eef

Cadbury Heath, an area east of Bristol
They don't make choclut in Cabry Eef mind.

Cacks

Underwear
What, ee ain't got no cacks on?

Camrawl

Camera
Jew bring yer camrawl?

Canave

Can I Have
Canave one a they?

Cane Shum

Keynsham, a small market town south east of Bristol
Cane Shum? Thas not Bristle nor Baff.

Cas

Can
Cas ee jump that high?

Casn't

Can not
Yer, ee casn't put that down yer.

Caw

Coal
Do ee know if this ows is built on a caw mine?

Cawd   Cold
Iss bleeden cawd out yer!

Cawlcalater   Calculator
Cas I borrawl your cawlcalater?

Chimley   Chimney
Has thee had thee chimley swept?

Chinawl   China
*Yer, watch ar muh's best chinawl
with that stick mind!*

Choclut   Chocolate
Ar muh don't like choclut mind!

Churz   Cheers
Churz muh!

Cinemawl   Cinema
*I seen your muh wiv ar ole man
down the cinemawl las night!*

Circler   Circular
I luvs petezawls cos they'm all circler.

Cliffun

Clifton, an affluent area of North Central Bristol
Iss posh up Cliffun mind!

Cocker

Friend
Awlrite me old cocker?

Colsnawl

Colston Hall
I seen Shakin Stevens down Colsnawl las week.

Concord(e)

A supersonic Bristolian aircraft not bought by the Americans
Ar ole man worked on concord.

Cookumer

Cucumber
Muh! I dint want no cookumer wiv me salid!

Coopeyen Down

Bending over / Crouching down
I was coopeyen down and the dog bit me ass.

Coors

Of course
Coors I luvs im, ee buys I chips.

Corried

To be deprived of normal automotive control
(f. The Coronation Tap, Clifton)
That glider got I right corried!

Counsawl Ows

A large building on College Green
Liebree? Ee's down by the Counsawl Ows me babber.

Cudda

Could of
Ee cudda told I ee was comen.

Cum Off

To fall off something
I cum off me bike and got a gurt big scrage ere.

Cum Tight

Painful/To hurt
Ow you basdurd, that cum tight!

Cuntray

Country
I luvs liven in the cuntray.

Custurd

Custard
Got any a that choclut custurd?

Cyclepaff

A murderous nutter
Stay away from ee, ee's a cyclepaff!

Dap/Daps Run / Nip or Plimsolls (Derived from Dunlop Athletic Plimsolls)
Dap down the shops ullee? / You needs daps to do PE.

Dapper A small child
It were all better when I were a dapper.

Darkside A former nightclub in Brislington; Parkside (derog.)
You ain't really gonna go up darkside?

Dats That is
Dats a good ideawl.

Dees Casn't Do Dat You can't do that
Oi! Dees casn't do dat yer!

Dedder / Dedun Corpse
Ee's a dedder.

Diarrheawl Diarrhoea
I got diarrheawl when I was down Asdawl.

Diesel Gettee	You will get a punch (clench fist whilst saying) *Diesel gettee if ee don't shut it!*
Dill	Deal *Jew get a good dill on im?*
Dinnum	Didn't they *They made a proper mess dinnum.*
Dint	Did not *I ast im but ee dint know nuffink.*
Discolated	Dislocated *Ee come off is bike and discolated is arm.*
Disn't	Did not *Yer, I disn't say ee could ave ee!*
Dissis	This is *Dissis all err stuff mind!*
Do / Do's	Does *Ee do's a proper job.*
Doggin Up	To look at threateningly *Ee's doggin I up.*

Dohnee	Doesn't he *Ah, ee looks evsa sad dohnee.*
Dollop	A lump of something *I'll jus ave a dollop of mash.*
Done	Did *Ee done that yeserday.*
Down	To *Weem goen down ar muh's later.*
Dowtown	Broadmead *or* The City Centre *Fancy comen dowtown fer a Steller an a fight?*
Drawlen	An illustration *I done this drawlen at school fer ar muh.*
Dreckly	Straight away *I went dreckly ohm.*
Drive	A bus / taxi driver *Next stop drive / Churz Drive.*
Drived	Drove *I drived ar muh down Asdawl smornen.*

A - Z

Dunny

Doesn't he
Ee looks jus like is muh dunny.

Dunt

Don't / Doesn't
Ar muh dunt like they cakes mind.

Dursn't

Dare not
*I dursn't go dowtown at night
no more.*

Eadfit

To lose your temper
Ee ad a right eadfit when ee sawl I broke it.

Eda

He does
Eda really luv that Fiestawl mind.

Eddlice

Headlights
Yer, yoom gone an left your eddlice on.

Ee

He / Him / This / That / It
Ee's a right nutjob ee is/Me ammer? Ee's over there.

Ee's A Bed

He is in bed
Ar ole man? Ee's a bed.

Eeuz

He was
Ee cudda told I eeuz goen out.

Eeve

He has
Eeve only told ar muh I was up the Gas mind!

El Dub

Lawrence Weston (LW), an area of North West Bristol
El Dub? Iss down past Wessbree, by Shire.

Elemm	Eleven *Be roun bout elemm an go dowtown.*
Embray	Henbury, an area of West Bristol *Embray? Thas where ar muh lives.*
Engrove	Hengrove, an area of South Bristol *Engrove? Thas where ar ole man lives.*
Eppy	Fit of madness / Headfit *She ad a right eppy when I tawd er.*
Er	Or *Oozee mean, ee er I?*
Erd	Heard *I erd your muh's a nutter.*
Err	Her *I told err no already.*
Evsa	Ever so *Ee's evsa ansum I reckon.*
Evun	Heaven *Fer evuns sake!*
Eyar	Here you are *Swannit do ee? Eyar then.*

Falled	To fall *I falled down an ole yeserday,* *scraged me ass.*
Famlay	Family *Ee gotta keep it in the famlay mind.*
Fanks	Thank you *Is that un fer me? Fanks!*
Fansay	Fancy *They cakes looks a bit fansay!*
Fawder	Folder *Stick ee in that fawder for I ullee.*
Feeder	The Feeder Canal *I caught ee down the Feeder, mind!*
Fer	For *Gif I it yer, I'll do it fer ee.*
Feud	If you had *Feud locked im ee uddent a bin nicked.*
Fick	Thick *Ee's a bit of a fick un in ee.*

Fiestawl	Ford Fiesta
	Ee got a Fiestawl XR2i. Iss gurt lush.
Fill-Un	Filton, an area of North Bristol
	They made Concord up Fill-Un.
Fin	Thin
	Ee's a smart diet, sheem as fin as ell.
Fine	Find
	Jew fine yer phone yeserday?
Fink	Think
	I bin finken about ee today.
Fire Up	To beat up
	You better go, ee wants to fire you up.
Florawl	A popular vegetable oil spread
	Swant florawl on ee luv?
Ford	Forward *or* Afford
	I look ford to it/I casn't ford it this munf.
Forn	A popular alcoholic cider drink; Blackthorn
	Anudder forn in yer fry Dave.

Fornbree

Thornbury, a small town north of Bristol
Yeh, I plays gawf up Fornbree.

Fotawl

Photograph
You got they oliday fotawls back yet muh?

Fought

Thought
I fought you said ee was lush?

Fowstay

Disgusting/Mouldy
I ain't eaten that it's all fowstay.

Fowzand

Thousand
It only cost I free fowzand pown.

Frages

For ages
Ar Dave? I ain't seenin frages now.

Framton Cotral

Frampton Cotterell, a small village north east of Bristol
This ain't bleeden Yate! Iss Frampun Cotral!

Free

Three
I got free of they now.

Frim

For him
I only got it frim

Frizz

For his
Iss jus frizz own amusment.

Froat

Throat
Smatter? Gotta sore froat?

Frontline

An infamous area of St Paul's;
Grosvenor Road
*Get they off a bloke down
the Frontline?*

Fru

Through
*Ee went right fru they cakes
like nuffink!*

Fruneral

Funeral
Jew see that fruneral? Ee was luverly.

Fry

For I/me
Awd dis un fry ullee.

Fur-err

For her
Ee said it was jus fur-err mind.

Furrplay   An exclamation of congratulations;
Fair Play
Thas yourn? Furrplay to you mate!

Furzday   Thursday
See you on Furzday.

Gas, The   Bristol Rovers Football Club
The Gas are at ohm tonight mind.

Gashead   A supporter of Bristol Rovers
football club
Yoom a gashead then is you?

Gawf   Golf
Swanna game a gawf?

Gawld   Gold
Wheres get they gawld yerrings?

Gay   Sad/Uncool
Them trainers is so gay!

Gibbim   Gave him/Give him
Jew gibbim your phone number?

Gif I It   Give that to me
Oi! Gif I it yer.

Ginormous   Smaller than gigantic but bigger
than enormous
They petezawls is ginormous!

Giss	Give me *Giss a drag on ee.*
Glenner	A person who is a couple of toppers short of a full loaf (Derived from Glenside Psychiatric Hospital) (derog.) *Ee's a right glenner mind!*
Glider	An alcoholic drink of fermented apples; Cider *Lav a pyeanhalf a glider luv.*
Goa	Go to *I gotta goa bed now.*
Gob / Gobbed	Spit / Spat *That basdurd jus gobbed on I!*
Goes	Going *I goes on me olides next week.*
Golnill	Golden Hill, an area of North West Bristol *They still built that Tesco up Golnill mind!*

Gonna

Going to
Ee's gonna get it when I gets awld of ee.

Gotta

Got to
Yoom gotta do as ee says, ee's the boss.

Grampfer

Grandfather
Ar grampfer gave I a tenner.

Grampfer Grey

Woodlouse
Jew see the size a that grampfer grey?

Granner

Grandmother
You stayen wiv I or goen with your Granner?

Guddun

A good one
Ee's ell of a guddun ee is.

Guff / Guffed

To break wind
Blige! Ast thee guffed?

Gurls

Girls
Jew see they gurls las night?

Gurt / Gert	Very
	Them shoes is gurt macky.
	Ow bigs your bleeden feet?
Gurt Biggun	SS Great Britain
	I went down the Gurt Biggun
	wiv scaw.
Gwahn	Go on
	Ah gwahn, please.
Gwahn En	Go on then
	Goen? Gwahn en.
	Ee won't be mist by I.

This section has been left intentionally blank as no Bristolian ever pronounces the letter 'H' at the start of a word.

A - Z

I

I have *or* Me
I bin out all day wiv ar muh/
That belongs to I.

Ideawl

An idea
I got an ideawl, get that un.

Ijut

Idiot
Ee's a bleeden ijut ee is!

Ikeawl

A large Swedish furniture store
I got ee down Ikeawl, smart innit.

Ill

Hill
They got loads a big ills in Briz.

Im

Him
Thas im there.

Inchew

Aren't you
Yoom a bit fick inchew.

Innit

Isn't it
Thas a bit big innit?

Innum

Isn't it / he / she *or* Aren't they
Ark at they, they'm full a crap innum.

Int Is / Am Not
Ee's a bad un int ee/I int goen dowtown.

Ippadroam Bristol Hippodrome
Jew see that panto down the Ippadroam?

Is His
Oi! Dats is dinner notchores!

Ise I am
Ise goen dowtown awlrite?

Iself Himself
Ee do's it all iself.

Iss It is
Snot mine! Iss ar Dave's.

Itchy-Barry Bristolian derivative of 'itchy-chin'. Declaration of disbelief
You snogged err? Yeah, itchy-Barry!

Jammer   Somebody who is very lucky
                Ee's a jammer.

Jammy   Lucky
                You jammy git.

Jan   Tramp (derog.)
                Jew get that coat out the bin?
                You steppy jan!

Jasper   Wasp
                I got stung by a jasper.

Jeerme   Did you hear me?
                *You ain't goen out atawl
                now, jeerme?*

Jew   Do/Did you
                Jew know where ee be?

Jigsawl   Jigsaw
                I done this gurt macky jigsawl today.

Jitter   A person with long hair (derog.)
                Ee's a right jitter ee is.

Kangsood   Kingswood, a town north east of
Bristol
Chasers? What up Kangsood?
Nah, I don't wanna ave a
fight tonight.

Keener   Somebody who works hard (derog.)
Ee done all his ohmwerk, ee's a
right keener.

Kiddie   Boy / Youth
(anything up to mid-twenties)
What im? Ee's just a kiddie.

Kinave   Can I have
Kinave one a they?

Koffay   Coffee
Comen back fer a koffay?

Lackey Band   Elastic Band
                    Ee flicked I wiv a lackey band.

Laff   Laugh
                    We was jus avin a laff.

Lamminutt   Laminate
                    Ar floors is all lamminutt now.

Laters   See you later
                    You off? OK, laters.

Largurr   Lager beer
                    Lav anudder largurr yer darlen.

Lav   I will have
                    Lav one a they ta.

Lease   Least
                    At lease I dint say nuffink!

Lectric   Electric
                    *Yoom got one of they lectric
                    tuffbrushes?*

Led   To lie down (past tense)
                    I bin led down all day.

Leebim / Leebem	Leave him/them
	Leebim alone, ee wunt
	doen nuffink.

Leebim / Leebem   Leave him/them
*Leebim alone, ee wunt
doen nuffink.*

Leevellen   Evening
Is ee goen out tomorrawl leevellen?

Lemerlade /   Lemonade
Lemnade   *Ar muh brung I some lemerlade
and it were lush.*

Lend   Borrow
Can I lend a pound off ee?

Lent   Borrowed
*I lent ar my muh's car off
err yeserday.*

Les   Let us
We goen then? Yeah, well les go.

Lessaf   Can I have
Lessaf a look at ee.

Lesson   Less than
Muh, you da give I lesson you gave err.

Lidawz	German budget supermarket chain; Lidl *She works down Lidawz now mind.*
Liebree	Library *I got loadsa books out the liebree.*
Like	*See Pronunciation Guide*
Lissen	Listen *Jus lissen to ee, ee finks ee da know it all.*
Lit Lun	A young child *Thee casn't even smack a lit lun no more.*
Look	*See Pronunciation Guide*
Lush	Very nice *That sandwich was gurt lush.*
Luverly	Lovely *Jew see er? She looked luverly.*
Luvver	Friend/Mate (non sexual) *Churz me luvver.*

Macky

Very big
Your feets macky.

Marnen

Morning
I see thee in the marnen then.

Masarge

Massage
Comen down the masarge parler?

Maul, The

The Mall, a large shopping centre
at Cribbs Causeway
Jew get they daps up the Maul?

Mauve Yer

I'm over here
Where am I? Mauve yer look.

Mawday

Mouldy
They cakes is all bleeden mawday!

Mazen

Amazing
No way! Thas bleeden mazen!

Me

My
Me head's killen.

Meader

A resident of Southmead (derog.)
Shaint goen out wiv a meader is she?

Mem, The	The Memorial Stadium *Ise goen up the Mem, comen?*
Member	To remember *Member that that bird you pulled up Chasers? Wot a munter!*
Mentalist	To be mental / mad / psychologically disturbed *Ee's a bit of a mentalist mind!*
Meself	Myself *I got one a they meself.*
Miat	My hat *I left miat on a bus.*
Mied	My head *I twatted mied on the floor.*
Mind	*See Pronunciation Guide*
Mint	Very good *Thas mint! Cheers!*
Moron	More than *They bleeders give us moron we could handle.*

A - Z

Muh	Mother *Ar muh got the dinner on.*
Munf	Month *Ise goen on me olidies next munf.*
Mungry	I am hungry *Muh mungry, whas fer tea?*
Munt	Not very nice *Muh, I ain't eaten they!* *They cakes munt!*
Munter	A person who's not very attractive (derog.) *I wouldn't touch err, she's a* *right munter.*
Murr	Mirror *Ave ee looked in the murr smornen?* *Yoom a right state.*

A - Z

N

Nawl Wess   Knowle West, an area of South
Bristol
*Snot rough up Nawl Wess! Iss
bleeden luverly.*

Nebbersin   Never seen
I ain't nebbersin ee round yer.

Needawz   Needles
I got pinz an needawz agenn!

Needs   Require
You needs a bath, you stink.

Neever   Neither
Ee dint see I neever.

Neffam   Netham, a steep hill leading to the
Feeder Canal
*I bin fishen down the Neffam. Never
got nuffink mind.*

Nellzee   Nailsea, a town west of Bristol
*I'd rather live out Nellzee than up
Widdywud.*

Nerr   Never
You dint win? Nerr mind.

No

Not
Fancy goen out then or no?

Notchores

Not yours
Dats notchores so leave it alone.

Nowse

Knows
Ee nowse where to find I!

Nuffink

Nothing
We wunt doen nuffink.

Nuh Night

Goodnight
Nuh night darlen, I'll see thee tamorra.

Nurlay

Nearly
Mind! Ee nurlay knocked me steller over.

Of

Have
I could of brung it home but I dint.

Off Of

Off
Where do ee get off of a bus en?

Oh Ah

I understand/Oh yes
Oh ah, I knows ee.

Ohm

Home
I bin sat ohm all day.

Olides

Holidays
Ee bin on is olides.

Ondawl

Honda
Ee got one a they smart Ondawl Civics.

Oo

Who
Right, oo called I a bleeden munter?

Oops

Hoop style earings
Is they your bird's gawd oops?

Ooze

Who is
There ain't nobody ooze fer the war ere.

Oozee

Who does he
Oozee know down ere?

Oozeefink

Who does he think
Oozeefink ee is?

Ore Field

Horfield, Bristol's prison /
an area of North Bristol
Ar ole man's in Ore Field.

Osbidal

Hospital
*I bin up the osbidal wiv ar muh
all night.*

Ow

How *or* Out
*Ow'd ee do dat? / Look ow, ansum,
yer she comes.*

Ow Bist?

How are you?
Awlrite? Ow bist?

Pacifically   Specifically
Ee pacifically said to put it yer.

Painen   Giving pain / To be in pain
*I gotta see a dentist, me tuff's
painen I rotten.*

Pardunn / Parn   Pardon
Parn me luv, I jus guffed

Parler Tawk   Former Bristolian hip-hop crew;
Parlour Talk
*Erd that Padlocked Tonic? Them
Parler Tawk blokes is mint.*

Pataytawls   Potatoes
Jew get they pataytawls down Asdawl?

Peepaw   People
*Ee knows loads a ard
peepaw mind!*

Pennety   Penalty
The ref gave I a pennety.

Petezawlut   A popular pizza restaurant;
Pizza Hut
We's all goen down petezawlut mind.

Petrawl   Petrol
Ave ee got nuff petrawl to get dowtown?

Pewjoe   A French car manufacturer
Blige, jew see that pewjoe?
Ee was lush!

Picka   Pickle
Cheeze n picka for I!

Pigsty III   An area of Gloucester Rd known
only by residents and bus drivers.
Ore Field Prison? Yeah, thas up by
Pigsty III.

Pirates, The   Bristol Rovers Football Club
The Pirates aint doen well this season.

Pitchen   Settling Snow
Look, the snow's pitchen outside!

Pitcher   Picture
She ad a gurt lush pitcher on err wall.

Plasterscene   Plasticine
Ar lit luns maken a morf outta
plasterscene.

Pot Nuda Pot Noodle
Got any a they curry pot nudas?

Pown Pound
Jew get ee down the pown shop?

Por'ersed Portishead, a coastal town near
Bristol
Por'ersed? What the group?

Praps Perhaps
Praps I'll go down town later.

Prawln Cocktell Prawn Cocktail
*Lav one a they prawln cocktells fer
a starter.*

Prittee Pretty
I luvs err cause she's real prittee.

Proper Excellent
*Them birds las night was
proper smart.*

Proper Job A job well done
Ee done a proper job on that kitchen.

Puddies

Hands
Blige! Me puddies is bleeden cawd!

Putnin

Put it in
Cas ee putnin there fer I me babber?

Puwher

Computer
Sat a new puwher? Smart un innit?

Pyeanhalf

A pint and a half
Pyeanhalf a Blakforn fer I Dave.

Pyjarmers

Pyjamas
Ar muh told I to put me pyjarmers on.

Q

Quicken

A fast one
Blige! Ee's a quicken innum!

Quipmant

Equipment
Ee got all the proper quipmant mind.

A - Z

Raggy   Hand rolled cigarette
                     Swanna raggy?

Rawl   A bread roll
                     They am rawls looks lush!

Razbrizz   Raspberries
                     They got razbrizz in them mind.

Replicawl   A copy; Replica
                     Don't buy ee, iss jus a replicawl.

Rit   Wrote
                     I rit to ar dad in Ore Field smornen.

Robins, The   Bristol City Football Club
                     The Robins is goen up!

Rown   Around
                     You dint walk rown town like that?

Rowna   Around the
                     Ee keeps is car rowna back mind!

Rus   Or else
                     Gif I it yer rus I'll belt thee!

Sabout
It's about
The vidjoe? Iss sabout some nutter.

Sadly Broke
Bradley Stoke, a recently built area north of Bristol
I got money, even though I lives up Sadly Broke.

Safternun
This afternoon
I ain't goen back a work safternun mind.

Saint
This/That is not
Yer Dave, saint rite is it?

Salid
Salad
Muh! I don't like salid, got any chips?

Saunawl
Sauna
Ee got one a they saunawls in is garden now.

Sawd
Sold
I sawd loads a they on ebay.

Sawl
Saw
I sawl it an I jus attle avit!

Scaw   School
                Goen a scaw safternun or not?

Scowen   Are you going
                Scowen ohm then or wot?

Scrage   To graze/scratch yourself
                I fell over an scraged me knee.

Scrumps   Small pieces of fried batter
                *When I goes down the chippy I
                always aves scrumps wiv me chips.*

Scud   A scab (as result of a scrage)
                I got a macky scud on me knee.

Scummy   Not very nice/Dirty
                See that kitchen, that was scummy.

Scutler   A promiscuous girl (derog.)
                What err? She's a right scutler.

Scutlers   Lambert and Butler cigarettes
                Gif I one a they scutlers.

See   *See Pronunciation Guide*

Seegaw	Seagull *Jew see that seegaw muh? Ee's gurt macky!*
Seen	Saw *I seen ee yeserday.*
Seenin	Saw him *Las time I seenin ee were up Chasers.*
Semm	Seven *Ee's goen out bout six or semm o'clock.*
Sex-ample	To set an example *Ee better sex-ample to they lit luns mind!*
Shag	A friend/mate *Awlrite shag!*
Shaint	She isn't *Shaint as good as she finks she is.*
Sheda	She does *Sheda get right on me tits she do.*

Shire	Shirehampton, an area of West Bristol *Shire's much nicer than El Dub mind.*
Shithead	A fan of Bristol City football club (derog.) *Me own muh's a shithead! I don't wanna believe it!*
Shoo-en	A beating *Ee's gonna get a right bleeden shoo-en when I sees ee!*
Shot Away	Mad / Insane *Twenny quid fer that?* *You gotta be shot away.*
Shrammed	To feel really cold *Shut them bleeden doors, I's shrammed in yer!*
Shup	Shut up *Will ee jus shup!*
Simler	Similar *Ee's simler to that un I got.*

Sint

Saint / St.
I lives down Sint Pauls.

Skelington

Skeleton
Yer, d'you see that skelington on the tele?

Skooze

Excuse me
Skooze, beers comen frew.

Skunna

It is going to
Skunna piss down later mind!

Sleever

A straight pint glass
Stick that forn in a sleever darlen.

Slider

Childrens playground slide
They got a slider down the park?

Smart

Very nice
That new mini's smart.

Smatter

What is the matter?
Smatter wiv err now?

Smoothen The Cat

Stroking the cat
I bin smoothen the cat.

Smornen	This morning *I got up smornen an she waz gone.*
Snell	Small slimy creature eaten by the French. *Don't step on any a they snells mind!*
Sno	Do you know *Sno anyone who do know?*
Snot	It is not *Snot mine! Iss ar muh's.*
Soufmeed	Southmead, an area of North Bristol *Snot Soufmeed! Iss Wessbree!*
Spanner	An idiot *Don't be a spanner!*
Spawnay	Lucky *Ar muh always wins, she's so spawnay!*
Spect So	I expect so *Muh, can I ave petezawl fer me tee? Spect so.*

Spenshun	Suspension *We bin up the Spenshun bridge all day.*
Spensive	Expensive *They daps is evsa spensive.*
Speshly	Especially *I made it speshly for you me babber.*
Spinner	Liar *They ain't yours you bleeden spinner!*
Spit	It is a bit *Spit crap innit?*
Spooner	Somebody who is not very bright (derog.) *Man, ee's a right spooner.*
Spoony	Uncool *Them shoes is a bit spoony.*
Spose	I suppose *Spose I gotta ave a go now anneye.*
Spreethed	Rough cracked skin through cold *It wunaff cawd! Ar ands got all spreethed.*

A - Z

Stayshun	Station *Do ee know where temple meads stayshun is?*
Steller	A popular lager beer; Stella Artois *Get I anudder steller Dave, but don't spill it mind!*
Stingers	Stinging Nettles *Muh, I fell in they stingers!*
Summut	Something *I ad summut simler meself once mind.*
Sumpfen	Something *I gottle get ar muh sumpfen for err birfday.*
Sunner	A male friend/mate (non sexual) *Awlrite me ole sunner, ow bist?*
Swant / Swanna	Do you want? *Swant I to do that?*

Swannee

Do you want this?
(usually asked when brandishing a fist or weapon. A threat)
Swannee er wot?

Swellead

An arrogant smug self satisfied person
Oooh ark at ee, gurt swellead.

Swemmen

Swimming
Comen swemmen?

Swot

It is what
Swot ee deserves mind!

Syew

It is you
Tis innit? Syew! I fought so.

Ta
To
Tell I when wedda get ta where ee is.

Taardown
Totterdown, an area of South Bristol
Glasnost in Taardown? Thas gurt lush up there.

Taint
It isn't
Taint alf ot muh.

Tamorra
Tomorrow
Ee be goen dowtown tamorra mind.

Tawd
Told
I tawd err straight, I bleeden ates you I said.

Tawk
Talk
I don't wanna tawk bout it no more.

Thas
That is
Thas right, we was there all day.

That Ain't Right
Is that correct?
I erd you got the sack, that ain't right?

The Kiddies
The best
Weem the kiddies!

| **Thee** | You |
| | *Why casn't thee go down the shop?* |

| **Them** | Those |
| | *Them daps is lush, wheres get em?* |

| **Theys / They'm** | They are |
| | *They'm just gonna be a pain in the ass.* |

| **Thur** | There |
| | *Ee was gone when we got thur.* |

| **Thuther/Tuther** | The other |
| | *Gif I tuther one muh.* |

| **Tight** | Mean |
| | *Yer, don't be so tight, gif im some of yours.* |

| **Tisunt** | It is not |
| | *Iss tonight innit? Tisunt! Snot till tomorrow!* |

| **Tis** | It is |
| | *Thas notchores! Tis. Taint. Tis. Whatever.* |

To

Used as a reference to a location.
Wheres that to? Where you to?

Toon

To him
I said toon, ee casn't ave it!

Topper

The end piece of a loaf of bread
*I don't want no toast with
toppers mind!*

Trimens

Christmas decorations
*Muh, whens we gonna get the
trimens up?*

Tuff

Tooth
I bin down the dentist to ave me tuff out.

Tuffbrush

Toothbrush
*I got a new tuffbrush down
Asdawl today.*

Tump

A small grassy Hill
Watch I rawl down this tump.

Tunawl

A large tasty fish in a can
Blige, that tunawl rawl's gurt macky!

Turbo Island   A small patch of grass in Stokes
                     Croft frequented by white cider
                     drinking street folk.
                     *They likes their zider up Turbo
                     Island mind!*

Turkay   Turkey
                     I luvs turkay at Chrizmuz.

Turnt   Turned
                     You shoulda turnt left not right.

Twas   It was
                     That wunt yourn!
                     Twas you glenner!

Twasnt / Twant   It was not
                     Twasnt fer ee I said!

Twat   To hit
                     Ee twatted im wiv a bottle.

Twenny   Twenty
                     Lav twenny a they.

Twot   Too hot
                     Blige, iss twot in yer!

Ulbum   A collection of musical tracks on one disc
You erd that new Por'ersed ulbum? Iss mint!

Ullee   Will you
Jus bleedin shut up ullee!

Uddent / Unt / Ussent   Wouldn't
I uddent mess wiv ee mind. Ee's ard!

Un   One
I got gurt big un.

Ungray   Hungry
Is ee ungray? Swant some tea?

Up   To
Jus goen up the shops muh awlrite?

Up The Downs   Going to / On Durdham Downs
I ad err up the downs.

Urrlay   Early
I aint getten up that urrlay mind!

Urt   Pain
Bleenell that urts!

V

Vawlse Vase
Jus stick they flowers in that vawlse.

Vegabull Vegatable
Do ee ave vegabulls with petezawl?

Vench Adventure playground; notably
Lockleaze
Comen up the vench?

Verrewkawl Verruca
*Thee casn't goa swimen baffs wiv
a verrewkawl.*

Vidjoe Video
Jew set the vidjoe?

Virrickawl Vehicle
I drives a public service virrickawl.

Volly, The A public house on King Street;
The Naval Volunteer
Wanna pint down the Volly?

A - Z

Wackum   To hit somebody
Did ee wackum?

Wall   Wool
Muh, got any cotton wall?

Wallop   A hit
Ar ole man's gonna give I a right wallop later.

Wanna   Want to
Wanna go dowtown?

Warter   Water
Muh, canave some warter?

Wassat   What was that
Yer, wassat noise?

Wasson   What is on
Wasson the tele muh?

Wayten   Waiting
I bin wayten frages already!

Was   Were
We was over there.

Weeda We do
Weeda always go up the Mall at the weekend

Weem We are
Weem in a right mess now.

Wells Wales, a country close to Bristol
They likes they sheep over Wells mind!

Went A Pisser To fall badly
Ar Clives muh tripped up the stairs and went a pisser.

Were Was
Ee were full of crap.

Werk Work
I bin a werk safternun anneye

Wernit Wasn't it
Top do las night wernit!

Wessbree Westbury-on-Trym, an area of North West Bristol
Snot Soufmeed! Iss bleeden Wessbree!

Wesson	Weston-super-Mare, a coastal resort on the Bristol Channel *Fancy aven some chips down Wesson?*
Wester	A resident of Knowle West (derog.) *Don't mess wiv a Wester mind.*
Whas	What are/do (you) or What is *Whas up to? / Whas fink? /* *Whas up wiv ee?*
Whas Ee Chatbout?	What is he talking about? *Whas ee chatbout? Sawl bleeden rubbish.*
Whas Fink?	What do you think *Whas fink of ee then me babber?*
Whas Mean?	What do you mean *Whas mean ee dunt wonna go?*
Whas Want?	What do you want *Whas want me to do bout it?*
Whasser	What is the *Whasser bleeden point?*

Where You To /
Where Bis?

Where are you
I casn't find ee, where you to?

Where Weetoo?

Where are we
Where weetoo now muh?

Wheres

Where have / did you
Wheres gettee?

Wheres Attoo?

Where is that
Baff? Wheres attoo?

Wheres Bin?

Where have you been
Wheres bin all day?

Wheres Eetoo?

Where is he
I knows ee's yer the basdurd!
Wheres eetoo?

Wheres Gettee?

Where did you get that
Smart fotawl a Concorde, wheres
gettee to?

Wheres Goen?

Where are you going
Wheres goen to muh?

Widdywud	Withywood, an area of South Bristol *Do this bus go up Widdywud?*
Widjew	With you *You bring that game widjew?*
Will	Wheel *Jew sells wills?*
Will Barrel	Wheelbarrow *I done me gardnen wiv a will barrel.*
Wimmilill	Windmill Hill, an area of South Bristol *Whas mean there aint no wimmill up Wimmilill?*
Windawl	Window *Yer, open them windawls will ee?*
Wiv	With *Whas avin wiv your chips?*
Wobby	What are you *Wobby on about?*
Wonna	Want to *Wonna go dowtown?*

Wudjew

Would you
Wudjew go out with my mate?

Wunaff

Wasn't half
Ee wunaff good looken!

Wunt

Was not
I wunt even gonna do that!

A - Z

X

Xterr   Exeter, a city in Devon
Cas ee get a Xterr on this un drive?

Yawl

You will
Yawl get me fist if thee ain't quiet.

Yer

Hey / Excuse me *or* Here *or* Ear
(singular)
*Yer you seen ar little un? Yeah ee's
over yer.*

Yer Awl

Earhole
Ow many studs you got in that yer awl?

Yer Tis

Here it is
Your wallet? Yer tis.

Yerrens

Earings
*Thems nice yerrings, is they
gawld-plate?*

Yeerin

Hearing
Ee needs is bleeden yerrin testen.

Yers

Ears
Sabout time you cleant yers out.

Yeserday

Yesterday
*I went dowtown yeserday,
I ain't goen safternun.*

Yewar

Here you are
Yewar ave this un ee's better.

Yewman

Human
Ee's only yewman mind!

Yoom

You are / have
Yoom right clever you is / Yoom left your wallet ohm?

Yourn

Yours
Zat yourn?

Yuey

UWE,
(University of the West of England)
A former polytechnic on the outskirts of the city
Oh, yoom only at the yuey.

Yungun

Somebody younger than yourself
Awlrite yungun, ow bist?

Zackley   Exactly
Thas zackly right!

Zat   Is that
Zat un youn?

Zider   An alcoholic drink of
fermented apples; Cider
Zider I up landlord!

A - Z

Phrases

1. Getting Around

Why is it there is no driver for this vehicle?
Wheres a bleeden driver to?

Would this service take me to the city centre?
Do this un go dowtown?

I wish to leave your vehicle at the next available authorised stopping point please.
Next stop drive.

Excuse me driver, could you possibly provide me with change from a twenty-pound note?
Yer drive, cas ee change this un?

No, I'm terribly sorry, I do not wish to accept a change ticket.
Whas I sposed to do wiv ee?

Sir, do you think this vehicle will be leaving soon?
Ullee be goen soon drive?

This service appears to running extremely late.
Blige, wheres bin?

I say, where exactly are we?
Where we to?

Excuse me young sir, you appear to be getting into my Taxi.
Yer yongun, dees better get out a there or diesel gettee.

I'm sorry to have to tell you children, but the upper floor of this vehicle is non-smoking.
Oi! Put they bleeden fags out or I'll tell thee ole man.

By Jove, you have appeared to place your motor vehicle into such a position that reversing it may prove problematic.
Yer, thee's got'n where thee casn't back'n hassen't?

2. Eating Out

Proprietor, I wish to purchase a pint of reassuringly expensive Belgian lager.
Pint a Steller me ole babber.

Please can you furnish me with your wine list?
Zider I up lanlord.

Barmaid, please could I have one more.
Gif I anudder un in yer darlen.

Please can you pass on my compliments to the chef as my meal was outstanding.
Yer mate, that was gurt lush!

Can you direct me to the local patisserie?
Wheres Greggs to?

I say, that tuna baguette does appear awfully large.
Blige, dat tunawl rawls gurt macky.

Would it be possible to sample a selection of your delicate pastries?
Gis I a steak bake anna sausage rawl me luvver.

Excuse me, I think you will find there is a mistake in this bill.
Yer, yooms tryen to rob I blind you basdurd!

Do you think I could have a rather large portion of mashed potato?
Gif I a gurt macky dollop of ee ullee?

Can you tell me, is there a traditional Italian restaurant close to here?
Wheres there a petezawlut rown yer?

3. Health

Excuse me Doctor, I believe my mother is suffering from psychiatric problems.
Yer Doc, ar Muh's shot away.

My father is suffering chest pains and may require urgent medical attention.
Get ar ole man to the ospidal, ee's aven an arrtack.

I have a infection, please can you inform my family.
I got an itchy box, cas ee call ar muh fry.

I have been feeling rather unwell and I believe my bowels may be loose.
I fink I got diarrheawl.

I'm sorry, you must be mistaken, I simply cannot be pregnant.
Shut up! I dint even do it wiv im!

I have had a toothache for some time now.
Me tuff's been painen I frages.

Following an altercation with my sibling, I believe I may have injured my testicles.
Ar bruvver jus kicked I in me baws!

I appear to be suffering difficulty breathing and require medicine to correct it.
I got asthmawl, gif I a puff on ee.

I am suffering greatly from pain due to inflamation.
Bleenell, iss gurt macky!

The lively discussion concerning taxi queue etiquette ended rather abruptly.
I fink me jaws discolated.

Excuse me kind sir, I believe my sight to be failing me.
Yer, I casn't see a bleeden fing. Not nuffink mind!

She appears to have lost an awful amount of weight, are you sure she is not suffering from anorexia?
Blige, sheda look like a right bleeden skelington!

I say, can you see the large stomach on that gentleman?
Look at the gurt macky gut on ee!

Please help me, my mother fell from a great height.
Yer, ar muh went a pisser down the stairs.

Could you please call me an ambulance?
Cas ee get an amblance fry?

4. Nightlife

Hello Miss. Whilst I don't think your friend is particularly good-looking, I do find you rather attractive.
Awlrite darlen! Your mate's a right munter, but yooms evsa prittee.

By golly, you are a fine-looking hunk of a man.
Blige! Yoom an ansum basdurd.

If you would like to buy me a drink of quality cider I may be able to entertain you.
Get I a Blakforn an ee cas gif I a quicken.

Would you like to come back to my residence for a spot of light supper?
Fansy a pot nuda round at our muh's ows?

David, do not entertain this fool's penchant for violence.
Leebim Dave! Ee aint wurf it!

Kindly take your hands from me or I will be forced to take action.
Get off I, or I'll stick thee in the bleeden BRI.

By jove the music in this venue is awfully loud, don't you think?
Blige, I casn't yer nuffink in yer.

Do you think you could direct me to an establishment where I may obtain light relief?
Do ee knows a good masarge parler rown yer?

I have to say that I was most entertained by the recent floor show I attended at the Colston Hall.
They strippers las night down the colsnawl,
they was gurt mint!

I would like to spend an evening at an establishment frequented by promiscuous young ladies.
Do ee know where the Horny Crumpet is to? I yerd iss fulla right scutlers.

I find your physical appearance quite revolting.
Yoom a right macky munter.

5. Useful Everyday Phrases

Thank you
Churz

No thank you
Nah

I don't understand
What?

Good morning
Awlrite

Good afternoon
Awlrite

Good evening
Awlrite

How are you
Awlrite

Good night
Churz en

Can you help me with...
Cas ee gif I an and wiv...

Could you please hold this for me?
Cas ee awd ee fry?

Can I have...
Canave...

Where did you get that?
Wheres gettee to?

Listen to that
Ark at ee

I just had to have it
I attle avit

Where have you been?
Wheres bin?

What is it you would you like?
Whas want?

Excuse me...
Yer...

Do you speak English?
Whas on bout?

Where is it?
Wheres eetoo?

I am looking for...
Wheres eetoo...

Can you tell me...
Do ee know...

Where are you?
Wheres eetoo?

Where are you going?
Wheres ee bleeden off to?

I say, is it you who has broken wind?
Ave ee guffed?

I am terribly sorry, what is it exactly that you are saying?
Whas ee chatbout?

Could you please give me change for this twenty pound note?
Cas ee gif I change of this twenny?

How are you?
Ow Bist?

Quiz

HOW BRISTOLIAN ARE YOU?

Do you prefer the smell of gas to that of Swedish pine and meatballs? Can you tell when an 'L' is surplus to requirements? More importantly, does it really bother you when two roads normally miles apart miraculously become adjacent in an episode of *Casualty*? Unsure? Well maybe you need to take our highly scientific test to decide just how Bristolian you really are.

1. A work colleague mentions this weekend they will be 'Watching the Gas'. Are they:

a) Keeping a keen eye on their fuel consumption.

b) Going to watch Bristol Rovers.

c) Trying not to fart too much.

2. Do you describe the revamped city centre as:

a) A marvelously modern installation of urban architecture and design.

b) Crap.

c) A good place to get knocked over or have a fight.

3. Lower Clifton is:

a) A vibrant and artistic community in the shadow of the Clifton Suspension Bridge.

b) An area of Bedminster now inhabited by people who really want to live in Clifton but can't afford to.

c) Bernie Clifton's legs.

Quiz

4. You spot a bargain in *Trade It* which claims to be in Westbury-on-Trym. Do you:

a) Grab your car keys and head out in the knowledge that everybody there is a bit posh.

b) Forget it. You know it's Southmead really. Nobody in Westbury buys Trade It.

c) Trade-It? I've got a credit card and I intend to use it. Where's Argos?

5. You are sitting on a bus in the centre waiting for a new driver. Do you:

a) Wait patiently. I'm sure somebody will be along shortly.

b) Get off, because it'll be quicker to walk home to Withywood.

c) Try to hotwire it and earn some pocket money. Low bridge, where?

6. Bristol International Airport - is it:

a) A great local airport from which to fly on holiday.

b) Too windy, too far, too foggy, too expensive to park, and not in Filton.

c) In Bristol?

7. Banjo Island - is it:

a) An ironically bohemian guitar shop on Gloucester Road.

b) A rough part of Cadbury Heath where the bus stops.

c) A small island in the South Pacific, inhabited by George Formby impersonators.

8. When catching a taxi from the centre to Clifton, the driver goes via the M32. Do you:

a) Ask if he's on all night.

b) Catch a taxi from the centre to Clifton? You lazy git.

c) Snigger to yourself because you've got no money anyway.

Quiz

9. How would you address your father?

a) Pappa?

b) Ar ole man.

c) I don't know who he is (and nor does my mother).

10. When in a bar the barmaid offers to 'Zider you right up', do you:

a) Leave, mumbling something about not wanting trouble.

b) Ask "will that be forn or fatchers luv?"

c) Decline claiming to be happily married.

11. The Bristol Observer, is it:

a) An interesting read packed with local news that you would happily pay 20p for where it is not free.

b) An ad-laden news-free rag, shoved through your letterbox whether you want it or not, which is good for nothing but lining the budgie cage or wrapping chips.

c) A small man who stands on a hill in Somerset watching the city of Bristol through a telescope.

12. What one word best describes Bristol city centre weekend nightlife?

a) Cosmopolitan - typical of any large European city.

b) Kicking – quite literally.

c) Boomshanka.

13. If you had to describe your accent, who would you sound most like?

a) The Queen

b) An educated farmer/pirate

c) Is that with or without helium?

14. What is the Bristol sound?

a) Chattering over a skinny latte.

b) Drum and bass cider blues.

c) Arr.

Quiz

15. How would you describe public transport in Bristol?

a) I own a Mercedes convertible, and I have a driver. Public transport is for commoners.

b) An unreliable, overpriced, underinvested collection of second-rate vehicles, which will probably leave you stranded in Lawrence Hill.

c) Brilliant.

16. Do you listen to BBC Radio Bristol?

a) Yes. I find the topical debate well balanced, the music current and tasteful, and the telephone callers absolutely riveting.

b) Only for the football when I can't afford to go.

c) I own a microwave.

Mostly A's - *Johnny Foreigner*

You have little hope in passing yourself off as Bristolian, even if you don't speak. You have no concept of what it is like to have the history of generations of sailors in your blood, and you probably never venture far past Clifton Down Shopping Centre. Maybe you should move back to Reading.

Mostly B's - *Truly Shipshape*

You are a true Bristolian, despite your location of birth. You are as native as the mud in the Avon. You probably buy the Evening Post every day, but wonder why. It is people like you that keep this city alive. We salute you me babber.

Mostly C's - *Space Cadet*

If Bristol was on Mars you would still be miles out. You just have not got a clue have you? Either you have never actually visited the city, or you reside in one of those expensive Legoland flats on the side of the floating harbour. Either way, there is not much hope of you ever becoming a Bristolian.

Quiz

If you hear a new Bristle word or phrase you think should be included in the next edition of the Dictionary, why not make a note of it on the following pages and then email it to:

richard@tangentbooks.co.uk

and you could make it into print!

Please put **ave ee** in the subject line.

Churz

I URD THISSUN

AN THISSUN

AN THATUN

I URD THISSUN ANAWL